Lift Every Voice and Sing

Lift Every Voice and Sing

by James Weldon Johnson

illustrated by Bryan Collier

Amistad

An Imprint of HarperCollinsPublishers

Amistad is an imprint of HarperCollins Publishers.

Lift Every Voice and Sing
Illustrations copyright © 2007 by Bryan Collier

Manufactured in China.
All rights reserved. No part of this book may be used or reproduced in any manner whatsoever without written permission except
in the case of brief quotations embodied in critical articles and reviews. For information address HarperCollins Children's Books,
a division of HarperCollins Publishers, 1350 Avenue of the Americas, New York, NY 10019.
www.harpercollinschildrens.com

Library of Congress Cataloging-in-Publication Data is available.
ISBN 978-0-06-054147-7 (trade bdg.) — ISBN 978-0-06-145897-2 (lib. bdg.)

Typography by Carla Weise
1 2 3 4 5 6 7 8 9 10
❖
First Edition

This book is dedicated to the

Karen Thomas and Marion P. Thomas

Charter School in Newark, New Jersey.

—B.C.

Lift every

voice and sing

Till earth and heaven ring,

Ring with the harmonies of Liberty;

Let our rejoicing rise

High as the listening skies,
Let it resound loud as the rolling sea.

Sing a song full of the faith

that the dark past has taught us,

Sing a song full of the hope

that the present has brought us;

Facing the rising sun
of our new day begun

Let us march on
till victory is won.

Stony the road we trod,
Bitter the chastening rod,

Felt in the days when

hope unborn had died;

Yet with a steady beat,
Have not our weary feet

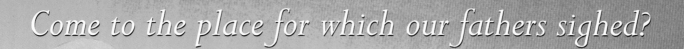

Come to the place for which our fathers sighed?

We have come over a way
that with tears has been watered,

We have come, treading our path
through the blood of the slaughtered,

Out from the gloomy past,
Till now we stand at last

Where the
white gleam
of our
bright star
is cast.

God of our weary years,
God of our silent tears,

Thou who hast brought us

thus far on the way;

Thou who hast by Thy might

Led us into the light,

Keep us forever in
the path, we pray.

Lest our feet stray from the places,

our God, where we met Thee;

Lest our hearts drunk

with the wine of the world,

we forget Thee;

Shadowed beneath Thy hand,
May we forever stand,

Lift Every Voice and Sing

This book is a celebration, a jubilee, and a song of hope through difficult times in American history, as well as in the present, in which people overcome the obstacles they experience in life. When Hurricane Katrina hit the Gulf Coast and New Orleans and the flood devastated so many lives, this text got louder for me. Water appears throughout the book in many forms—as an ocean that carries a slave ship to a New World, as a reflection pool with a statue of Dr. Martin Luther King Jr., and in water fountains that welcome everyone to drink from them. The faces of children singing to the heavens recur throughout the book, just as the faces that were caught in Hurricane Katrina cried for help and rescue, and their song reverberated throughout the world.

—Bryan Collier